SAND THEORY

SAND
THEORY

Poems

WILLIAM OLSEN

TRIQUARTERLY BOOKS
NORTHWESTERN UNIVERSITY PRESS
EVANSTON, ILLINOIS

TriQuarterly Books
Northwestern University Press
www.nupress.northwestern.edu

Printed in the United States of America

10 9 8 7 6 5 4 3 2 1

Library of Congress Cataloging-in-Publication Data
Olsen, William, 1954–
    Sand theory : poems / William Olsen.
      p. cm.
    ISBN 978-0-8101-5217-5 (pbk. : alk. paper)
    I. Title.
PS3565.L822S26 2011
811.54—dc22

                              2010038016

CONTENTS

III

ACKNOWLEDGMENTS

Grateful acknowledgment is given to the editors of the following periodicals, where some of these poems appeared, sometimes in different versions:

Blackbird:	"Light or Dark Speech"
Court Green:	"Essay on Craft"
	"Waking Slow"
Crab Orchard Review:	"Human Ashes"
Dunes Review:	"The Art of Goodness"
	"The Days After the Day of the Dead"
	"Last White-Throated Sparrow of May"
	"Long Distance Friends"
Epiphany:	"Voice Road"
Gettysburg Review:	"Lake Leelanau Goes Still One Day in Fall"
The Little Review:	"Good Night" (published as "The Waves")
New Ohio Review:	"Cabbages Across from the Manitou Islands"
Parthenon West Review:	"Dropping Off to Sleep"
Poetry Northwest:	"You"

| *Quarterly West:* | "Black Rot" |
| | "Dune Grass" |

| *Saranac Review:* | "Harvest Midnight" |

| *Shenandoah:* | "First Bible" |
| | "Leaf Watching, for Landor" |

| *Tiferet:* | "Theology of a Mosquito" |

TriQuarterly:	"Sand Theory"
	"This Heaven"
	"Those Yachts"

| *West Branch:* | "The Nonsighting" |
| | "Under Foot" |

"Grocery Night" was published in the anthology *Mentor and Muse: Essays from Poets to Poets* (Carbondale and Edwardsville: Southern Illinois University Press, 2010).

"The Last White-Throated Sparrow of May" and "The Days After the Day of the Dead" were reprinted in *The Rose Metal Press Field Guide to Prose Poetry.*

"The Last White-Throated Sparrow of May" was also published as a broadside by Michigan Book Arts Center.

"Light or Dark Speech" was reprinted in *Pushcart Prize XXXV.*

Thanks also to the Guggenheim Foundation and Western Michigan University for support that provided the time to write many of these poems.

SAND THEORY

No fact is isolate.

—LORINE NIEDECKER

I

Grocery Night

I have seen nothing that hasn't already been
lost from its birth
so many times the avenues have a sheen—
as a car passed through a car wash glows
from happening in the now, which isn't talking
in this city of snowmen
who lose their heads
and then their torsos
and even their nakedness.
And these same doors to needs
and to these shoppers
wheeling carts around,
and almost every time the same bagger
who shall remain nameless
pushing my groceries into the backseat,
as if to push his own
existence out of his hands and shut the door,
speaks in a voice fatigued by its own formality
the words for just how tedious it is
to buy this night and many like it,
we shoppers with sacks of perishable goodness
our heads moon above
with the borrowed light
of the streetlights and the car lights
spread across our features
carved at times as out of sheer inertia.
That light is changing like the money
we try to make all day and into night
to provision our lives
while our children roll another evening away
until it snowballs

to people with nothing but weather on their minds
shaped out of this snow,
still wearing handprints,
looking more and more like the mess
one life is not enough to face.
Landscape of demand and demand
and little lights of comprehension,
supply of saving graces,
the sacks of groceries in back
death cannot celebrate
and famine cannot touch,
as each engine turns over
like a sleeper and is gunned alive,
I look up from my hands on the wheel.
Behind each pair of car lights
there is a person or two, families
whole or broken,
workers all alone
warming their hands with their breath
in distances you must travel to believe,
merging with the bound—
this road, this wilderness—

Dropping Off to Sleep

My quarrel with my life understands me through and through.
It requires me to argue tonight with my absent friends,

colleagues, parents, enemies, talking heads, students
all going on and on like players in a stage rehearsal

till there is no one left in my entire life I haven't told off,
till the end of consciousness, which is unacceptable.

All the billions upon billions of untold indignities.
That half the world starves, the other half frets or gloats.

That even death and chaos have a right to be as they are.
Then ego recalls some withering remark or other; then

there's a thin unblown half-moon up in tossed trees
telling me I haven't even begun to experience distance.

For I have one more insult to make, a perfect comeback
to win over every jerk in my life and bring us all peace—

which I keep losing like the leaves must lose their trees.

This Heaven

This heaven feels homeless and requires love more than ever now,
as do the gangs of pigeons growing in numbers like the unemployed
and the foreclosed houses up and down Westnedge Avenue
themselves homeless and out of work, even the furniture looking evicted,
downcast shoppers at the downscale midtown grocery store
where all races meet like prizefighters on the head of a pin,
the angels we call clerks, one love, one life, one dread looking out of their
    kindness,
more angels along with me pushing empty cans into the giant machines
    of RETURN
not far from the red peppers stacked in pyramids like giant bloody molars.
I'm spooked that I relish living for those few suspended instants
when money changes hands and I find myself exchanging good wishes
with a person no less strange than myself.
In this heaven, that I am talking to myself so much is as heartbreaking
as the neighbor across the street who picks up every twig on her sidewalk
because secretly she wishes to put a tree back together.
Instead she gathers them one by one and in handfuls drops them
into a Yard Waste Only bin and goes on speechlessly living.
While I am somehow suspended between the verbal and the nonverbal,
especially when I am walking downhill to the grocery store.
Then people without cars look like pedestrian statues, arms to their sides.
They look like art might be winning the millennium.
What is it about these people, they look up at me sometimes as if they had
    heard a church bell,
then go back to trying to stare themselves back inside me, a person I know,
who for all his debased loneliness is preferable to a religion of brass.
He could be sitting next to a woman reading in a subway under any foreign
    city,
her book so close to her eyes he can almost hear the words.
The news today is how we will again be swept into history.

We will weep blood and beer and mud, we will have to walk away from all
   the forgotten.
Some of us will be ordered to stand frozen in our tracks,
some of us will spring leaks from standing in fountains,
some of us have been standing on pediments ever since this heaven began
   turning into stone
ordinary losers, ordinary winners, happy as me at times, with average cares,
Lotto faces, Lotto hands, Lotto-gray eyes rubbed clean for the exhilarations
   of the losing numbers,
all in this heaven where hope winds us up and we march around
because in this heaven hope can never get enough of itself.
Not in the train station with the ticketless bums and dopeheads and any others
changed not just utterly, as Yeats had it, but forever, by which I mean
mortally beyond daylit thoughts of elections and eternal revelations,
in the light of snow, under the available noon shadow of the Rickman House,
flushed out, sacked, sent packing from picturesque wooden benches,
looking like unoccupied movie extras in a docu-poem about poverty.
The camera stops wheezing and the writer and the readers fall asleep.
In a bar I like because my colleagues wouldn't think to go there, I find myself
   drinking iced tea
seated across a table set with two paper place mats that double as menus
from a student with the tattoo of a heavenly gun or cross or flower
or barbed wire up her arm all the way up a still-alabaster neck
telling me the money just think of the money blown on smack
only to give most of it away to anyone with a steel needle and a
   hummingbird's self-precise addiction,
looking from across the table at a hopelessly AWOL father figure.
My self, my dear, my poor entirely helpless excuse of a mentor.
All I can say since she can't afford the therapy that got me back on
   my feet
is read novels, and if you can't do that, watch movies, take an interest
in narratives other than your own and don't shut out your stupefying friends,
they need your love, they look up at you dumbly even when they talk down
   to you.
I err in my tacit reassurance to her that it is absolutely natural to err.

But her face also seems perfect, that is, unchangeable, stamped, locked,
one of the many perfectly unphased by success or failure or love or neglect
that I'd never really looked at, though I have all the time in the world
because the future is so busy despising itself, it can't remember how to
    destroy the present.
Because this afternoon is so brutally glorious who on earth could love it
    tenderly.
Because another afternoon will take me in when finally I walk outside,
lost in the tyranny of arbitrariness, listening for anything alive, like
that moan—some neighbor diving into a pool on a hot day, that sound
reaching out in the belief that there was life to reach out from.
Once, all things touched, that's the sound, that's how to say it.
Trees in full leaf, green darker than night, those like me with walking
    pneumonia
are sunset's candle flames, and the faux colonial door lights, when twilight
passes through my neighborhood on its knees, are supplicating
for some very end that ends all in-betweens and all lingerings.
Today I lingered to talk to the bagger with the stump for a left arm
who offered up an incompletion that once was loss and excruciation,
a tapering fingerless nothing of an arm that can slip between the paper handles
of a grocery sack while he looked up at me like *I* was incomplete,
I who still like to compare those banal porch lights to coal pressed into
    diamonds,
sensing as I do unbearable mountains of pressure on the self,
with nothing but spectacular gems of continuance in its mind
and its failures to talk to some neighborhood loony bird with clothes so
    tattered
they precede the art of tailoring, the sweatshops in garment districts.
In this heaven I dress in the naked light of my own naked thoughts.
This heaven has become a church on steel wheels, faces rustling by through
    concrete pastures.
Me thinking my student can have my happiness because I know it doesn't last,
because for this heaven to be I must believe that nothing lasts, not even the child,
not even the mother, not the father nor scripture nor scribe.
Nobody's god in this heaven, nobody's fool or servant, nobody, nobody.

That's where this heaven begins, ex nihilo, la via negativa, ne plus ultra.
Waitresses like travelers magically waft by. It is as if everyone could walk
straight through everyone and we do not have to understand the reasons.
That student, the words, there in the shadow of the valley of their making
where everything happens, bright drinkers, stymied teacher, his faltering
        advice—
it is all advice inside this heaven, the backyard shadow
advises a falling leaf to meet it halfway, take it slow, there, there, okay,
bar smoke advises the lungs to keep breathing anyway,
afterthought advises thought to slow down, thought advises afterthought
to shake a leg, feeling advises both to lower your expectations and just
sit there with your hands palm down like beached starfish
or holding a fork or flapping around like crows in an appalling moonlight
across from a young and serious woman whose troubles
are earthly, whose silence advises the least sound of silverware
it is okay to be outdone by the deafening.
All advice counts backwards from googol, advice itself is the point,
and that one right word of advice, whatever it is, sounds so good
it annihilates all subsequent words, so let's try to keep it to ourselves,
or even the darkness would be gone, the longlast summer's last long stifling
        breath.
The heat will hold for a week or two, until it is like talking into a shoe
whose return advice is keep walking, wear me down below earth,
keep at it, light the way, stand tall, stay gold, don't look back in sorrow,
clear your cheerful voice and say at present your past is a shambles,
try harder, but leave be the shadow of the valley of advice,
and know that no one ever hears her like she does herself.

for B

Harvest Midnight

Like a thankful sight
the moon comes out.
And the act of seeing it is there.
Yes I think it could be blown away

by a dying breath.
It could be given back to its creator
all comet scarred

as an incomprehensible lapse
in judgment
and all that would be missing
would shine,

the shy memories and the memories
agitating entire lifetimes for attention,
memories
the whole night over,

every wavering choice.

Light or Dark Speech

Reading this word and that word takes you somewhere else, and nobody toasts November around here. Watching words swim in low chair light calls back worms punctuating our summer patio, out of their element, plucked up by a friend less squeamish than I, squirming, tossed to the side—snapping in the air like hooked fish, then drooping over the pachysandra. This is to say, the words don't flood out, they crawl up, they go wherever they are flung, at least when I'm not thinking too hard about what I'm reading, sheltered in a cottage from winds that could tear the open book of the roof and throw it and its margins and its gutters across the street. Flashing backwards and forwards in blinking streetlights, that's as far-fetched as books fly. For all this I'm still only reading because reading is calm and dry enough. I could now fall back into the armchair of morbidity, which Browning said is worth the soul's study. I once told my mother in a dream you are dead and later Mary told me you are farther along than I am for I still have a feeling of respect for the dead. I am always telling my mother she is dead while she's always telling me off. Even when I'm reading she's reading me the riot act. Morbidity, worth the soul's study. And the least peaceable kingdom. That salmon I touched with the tip of a stick charred by a beach fire, sand glazing it, dead, out of time, and always in season. Yet there is still ambition on its face, not even cessation is rest. I am sad because the Bluebird closes by November. Because beer sounds are at least a company. Of many instant friends in many mirrors. Sadness is always human. Sluggish headlights in the rearview mirror, the past you just can't trust not to run you off the road. I told my mother she was dead. And she told me *You know how bubbles creep up the side of a glass, then, suddenly, pull off, start out, suspend on the surface then pop? What happens next I and they have escaped.* She never wrote me but a few letters. She spoke a lot, for, of, at, to, with me. Dark speech in the afternoons, light speech in the mornings. Now this wind—a consciousness upon a consciousness—this wind I was and am gets no good done. The time it takes to think to ask why passes. As for whether there should be a ceremony for her few lost letters, burn them once and for all and have the ashes scattered by hand, with hesitation, the way a feeling, before saying something, scrunches the face. I climb into bed with that face and read while the wind gets to its point, which is to make things move and tear things down without tipping its hand. I read and read until there is nothing but words, and the book falls to the floor like a roof to a house without floors or walls, a house of words, words that preceded me, words behind and ahead of me, before and after me, read in the light or spoken in the dark.

Human Ashes

Even if we are
      what we were,
our senses,

      our crying,
laughing,
      so many dawns,

such long nights,
      so many
dreams and wishes,

      even if fulfillment
betrayed longing,
      even if it didn't,

even if what we
      are is joy
that loves itself

      and sorrow
is a way of
      seeming free

from any vanishing,
      even if we are
creatures with pasts,

      beasts with prayers,
even if some
      lasting aspect

of our essence
        is beyond
its sad occasion,

        what part
was strong then, what
        part weak,

what part
        as a child
did I touch,

        whatever part
placed my head
        in its hands

and soothed me
        and whatever
part loathed

        the rest to death
doesn't anymore
        feel that discrepancy

between the fire
        and ash,
love or love lost.

The Art of Goodness

—for Jon Anderson

Till the dead rise in respect, they break down the glass house
in which it turns out that goodness, everyone's, lives,

and step across that broken glass, bless goodness with fortune,
but refuse, retracing bloody footprints, to eat its torment.

The art of goodness, utterly open, just as utterly private,
reminds me exactly who I am to say so. The art of goodness

passes on any laurels to others rather than wear them.
It lives alone, and sometimes dies from its own companionship.

Dumb luck is irreversible, no one dies well, so what.
Favorite teacher, no longer named Ease or Hardship,

dear Jon, that I love you means I must never be you.
I'm not certain of anything much, or whether I'm talking to you.

I've not the wisdom or grace to say I should even try.
But I believe in mortality even if I don't understand it.

I believe in it like nothing else I do. Still, I've been trying
to walk out of the body all my life . . . it doesn't *get* me.

Did you say loss is never at a loss for words? Did you say
loss doesn't like to be kept waiting, that it kills us?

It kills us all the time, which should be impossible.
It never departs, it only returns, it sees through us, it sees

everything for the last time, and still despises sentimentality. Dear memory, I can't lose you; I can't *afford* to lose you.

Dear friend, you are the precious loss that keeps on giving. . . . I'm not sorry to love you, I'm sorry to love you so distantly.

Dune Grass

It is what sand would look like if it could just
escape itself and grasp the diffuse and clump around
pilings like stumps of teeth ground by tide,
risen to whatever inhuman trial it is

to have threadbare wind for a coat and a body
that has no eyes and no face to love,
bent in scarcely rooted supplication.
When have we not seen it praying

in its own loose unison of piety,
in its strength to waver and stay put and outreturn
the hulking one-time-only beachfront condos—
I'll worship something that would return to all this.

Repeatedly this need to be somewhere real again
comes upon land with features that never settle,
this treasure so openly fragile it's beginning
to dawn on me that we should all be singing—

no place like this anywhere in the world,
even the ground one stands on taken up,
what it means to escape damnation and holiness
and be forever risen into being used

right here at my glowing naked toes.
We walk right over all this we love the sight of
that in it we can love our transience,
our hills, their lakes no older than our species,

as it turns out earth never belonged to itself,
till even despondency seems hopeful evasion.
So why this trust, this sudden drop from bluff
to lake where sky resides and spars of buried trees

are disinterred from dunes, the beached hulls
of ghost barns are open houses, bare rafters
almost fallen in on their blessed ghost cows?
Why do ears settle on lone islets of seething birches,

tremblings near an even vaster trembling?
For however much I meant to find a human likeness
down on its knees, its hands churched together,
there's more room than ever for the booming distances

and sand enough for wind to blow beyond
all of us who abandoned, betrayed, trampled repeatedly
haywire paths, shown nothing new, no, this,
right here where there is no dogma or heresy,

shimmering just a little above the earth,
in its strength to waver and yet stay put
lifted by sun and rain into being used,
hanging on and letting us come and go.

You

The hills the lakes the shorelines only
three thousand years old. Some faces
have this same settled freshness every time.
Few voices do. I have been trying to walk
out of my body all my life. The flesh
doesn't belong to itself. Not a breath
we can understand so why this trust?
Understanding itself is a shape-shifter.
Even if I must accept your mortality,
I stay in love like nowhere else I stay.

Good Night

I left an office lamp alive for ghosts,
let go any hope
so easily

and tried to sleep.
But sleep left me on
like a night-light.

Some passing car
would be seen on its way,
some lasting meteor

anyone can see
forever fall,
some moon like an unsent letter,

some long-distance glance
stare from the bottom of the deepest
fare-thee-well.

Dear self, please say the sun.
The sun sets.
Say the moon,

the moon rises.
All these years
don't bring it an inch closer,

no telephone back to childhood either.
All America,
good night,

sleep tight,
but not yet.
A few stars have no distance,

their arrangement is lenient,
a moon sawn in half,
that half hanging on,

a cleaver over every waker and sleeper,
what on earth can I do,
waves lapping out lake

good and all alone,
where are they going,
what have I done?

Through the trees
their audible transparence,
each wave

always the first and
ever the last,
a few boat lights rocking,

wide awake is motion,
all's to come and the ordinary wait
is a vast devotion but first,

Sleep, bless
any dreams
with merciful instruction.

The Nonsighting

Stars out there everywhere
    so long as you look up intently
        from this idea

of a village of happy-go-lucky smiles
    all asleep at the proper hour
        or tumbling in nightmare

and doing so discreetly.
    Stars out there where a blue towel
        has beached in a plastic lawn chair

all night as the night requires
    witness and testimony
        even from inert creation

though it looks languorous there,
    retains some obscure
        draping towards a purpose.

Which must be out there too.
    Which must tolerate
        the fortunate skeptics

who ride the high-octane exuberance
    of their nearly irrefutable
        position that there is

no position. As for the otherwise
    fortuned, the rest of us,
        as for all of the revisions we

mostly are and transcribe with
a cough or a kind glance,
I was there, so much a so-so solo

counting myself among all of the below.
And who watches *under* us?
A timer sprinkler's little wet speeches

among the rhododendrons
startled me with a 6:00 A.M.
greeting from the universe of habit,

universe of managed instabilities
among the day-numbered
last blossoms of the universe

of lastingness for as long as
lastingness
grinds us to grit.

I thought this outside noise a danger,
an exhibitionist or a voyeur,
some human identity

beyond the reaches of my comfort zone.
Then, a munching deer
was what I'd have had there

to give my insomnia an excuse,
embodied, antlered
with cathedral candelabra,

resting on top of each lit wick
a bird of ordinary paradise.
And then the visitor who was never there

was gone and nothing language says
    but says it anyway.
        Easy wind from the lake

was gnawing to sand what it wasn't
    tossing around, leaves
        thrown up like children's hands

having guessed the right answer
    for once because for once,
        because even if never again,

all the questions are true and false,
    armful by armful the wind
        detaching anything it can.

I'd like my life to be free of its source,
    the way leaves don't seem to miss
        unmoved trees.

I'd like to be as open as a window,
    see-through as silicon,
        until Everything entered . . .

so I raise that guillotine window
    and black-rot maple leaves
        whisper of being as innumerable

as the usual huddles of stars,
    swarming supernumeraries,
        which don't and do connect—

you know what I mean.
    You were asleep.
        Something that rustles can't be trusted

any more than these stars that are present
    and not, and in either case
        go on and on all blinding day.

A small crowd of celestial bodies.
    They might as well be huddled
        at a doorway.

The rest is out of the picture.

Theology of a Mosquito

A thorn for a mouth, thirst for belief
        and brevity for a god—
imagine putting that face on even a day.

Black Rot

Speaking of colors in transparent breath—
you get the idea how difficult it is.
I can paint you that difficulty,

the vacant maple across the vacant lot
a few shades closer to resplendent pumpkin
but most of it is gone

and won't be represented
and won't open a gate even to its own
broken palace.

If you look at a single leaf
you see the cause of premature autumn,
what passes early and without warning

sandblasted, facially pocked
this one that cups my attention,
this one that slams and slams its door

and never shuts.

———

I'm staring at a blighted leaf,
the blight staring back at me
when my father phones from his tidy sunlit

widowed domicile.
He's never wished me anything but well.
His voice crackling from age, still neatly

prearranged to happy formations of syllables,
tendering chiding questions—
the prerogative of old age,

what we have to wish and hope for, now—
now unrolling himself in partial
sentences, punctuating himself,

the selfsame prose he speaks,
and I hear compliance say it's beautiful here,
you should see it.

Just beyond the mansions that block any view
I could convey to minimize his grief,
gulls huddle so far inside themselves

they will never be other than interior—
I've been there, yes, done that, suffered
opacity for which no pigment exists.

And when he hangs up, my loneliness
feels habitable, lovable, not survivable
but what survives us as a matter of fact,

an heirloom, a gift his voice confers
and the thread of the phone wire travels the theme
that ties this fabrication to us,

the same one that unravels us.

———

And the leaves turn, I turn them,
my regard is boss—
one side pale green and ancient parchment brown,

the other fingerprinted by a coal miner,
three leaves with six or seven splotches each,
enough chance blemish to roll the dice on,

tar and oil brimming upon each leaf
margined by gold-colored light
like a beach that walks itself around a black lake.

Each leaf has been to Dis
and back and now the blackest footsteps show—
plucked from a beach where waves come on

like cascading boats with bubbles for cargo,
where human footprints, grown in depth and scale,
make it look as if a troop of Athenian statues

walked off their pedestals and practiced drills here,
water polishing stones to a dry dim light
all stone, light you could fashion into a home

which only shines should water bury it.

———

Autumn begins in us before it begins
in things as heat begins to wane,
with so much hope that sadness will pay out

all that it owes us for feeding on us.
It begins and it begins to end in us
before it ends while blades of grass

the color of overuse, yellowed but not yellow,
blow like razor-drawn wings across
a field of blown grass. *Holding on*

sounds pathetic in this endless shudder,
windblown trees sounding like sand
scouring across the shingles of a barn

like a shipwreck. Trees speaking like sand dunes
with branches, leaves, a crown, maybe a few shrewd nests,
description wants the substance of description,

father wants son to love the earth's
overwhelming and collective murder and he does,
because love makes the same *us* of us all around,

because in love we kiss the sand so sand
can't have power over us. And meditation—
what is the adverse relationship between it,

the evenly hovering psychological gaze,
and attention, the dive-bombing heron gaze
also action and never a need for a directorial cry

for action when all things down to their
roots in mystery find purchase,
and any design breaks to unbrokenness,

as late afternoon light breaks in a father's voice,
then recollects to break again as waves
show themselves refulgent when they do,

visible upon crash, like a leaf radiant
with disease, black eyed, all curled up like that,
like it's trying to go inside when there is

no inside while brittle sticks for legs
fold and gulls bed down like decoys
well before evening, they *feel* endings. . . .

———

That particular late afternoon color the lake takes on
when the sun, inarticulate from cloud,
still paves a path, a white glitter, an escalator

that goes and goes as long as have and hold.
It looks brilliantly obscured, grays, whites,
gray-blues all seen through a pane of thin

gray glass that would break if it could.
That *has* broken, shattered, dispersed
into sand, and, yes, compared to sky or lake,

a beach seems something altogether accessibly alien,
a place no astronaut has ever walked,
yet there are all the half-naked families and loners,

and enviable lovers whose hands arrange stones
to hearts and pebbles to spell out their initials,
on sand with an almost human give beneath the feet.

———

Drift after drift, wash out and in and sift.
"Of course we are challenging nature itself"
Herzog said in defense of dragging a boat

over a Peruvian hill as if the hill itself
were "vile, base, choking, fornicating, asphyxiating"
all the while even the camera fighting for *survival*,

which is what we call duration these days.
But doesn't each blackened leaf drift in a movie of tragic
proportions where every last extra

sits on a threadbare terry cloth throne
wishing the familiar afternoon well and better
and for clear sky long after any ever after

and the lake takes that sky on its back
and you look back to the past and walk up
a beach to get back there and the past

turns out to have been a contempt for the future.
An old man with a face like a kitchen pot
pokes through the sand for something

not taken for granted, another personable
sign that also suffers observation,
beach glass stellar at his New World feet

and each star and each leaf never a stray,
each black-splotched leaf is the bottom
of a well from which a gaze shows me my father's face.

Long Distance Friends

What have they gone to what have I done
or made them do to me to leave me alone?
Did I let them make me make them?
What on earth can I do to help them?
When will they creep like moonlight over stones?
When will they pick up the telephone?
Times they do call: more time between.
When I think of them asleep I pretend
they dream of me and wake, and comprehend
they rhyme with each other they rhyme
without cease they rhyme with the only
rhyme in the book that rhymes with lonely,
in the book of ages, in disappearing ink,
and, even stranger, fellow boat lights that blink
good night, good riddance, good and all alone,
rocking boat lights constancy would frown upon,
friends so far away night can't hold on,
or a day moon sawn in half, the best half gone,
clouds out of the lovely south all alone,
waves lapping up out of the lake alone,
and sails tacking out this has-been afternoon
clean as eyeteeth and friendly to no one,
what have they gone to what have I done?

Cabbages Across from the Manitou Islands

The earth is the subconscious of the subconscious.
—BACHELARD

I

Half a block inland and safe from genius gulls
local and alone in their dishwater droves,
up out of reach from beach inland-eaten

by gutless waves,
opposite the passage from two fresh green-furred
ursine islands, one lighthouse-flicker lit, one not,

safe from shark-toothed sails and trolling trolls,
unseen by one old crow
patrolling a fire-log-charcoal-pitted shore,

innocent, green, unschooled, dim-witted, featureless,
foregrounded by the imponderable plumpness
of the crimson mother ships, summer's end's tomatoes,

encephalitic, all intelligence,
stupidly, yet astonishingly so,

2

formation in a deer-protected pen,
each shaped of give and take, the tight-leafed *both,*
oblivious to the bee, the gnat, the moth,

earless, eyeless, tearless, softheaded clones,
sunlit, windblasted, morning-tear-misted,
unlobotomizable,

sauerkraut helmets un-shovel-hacked,
inmates of drizzle from glacial clouds,
or funereally suited in fog shroud,

unmonitored yet reconnoitered, so far inside
themselves they don't come back to the same
seek and hide

but leaf out lowly, frugally, loyally,
reality's verities: cloddish nobilities,

3

ordinary fames
loudspeakered by this papery voice, admittedly:

fondly, sanely and madly,
with or without outlook,

writing the dung book
on life before utility, before soup, salt, spoon,

giving their redolent all,
outdazzled by streetlight, starlight, even matchstick,

penned yet hardly bound,
not yet lost not yet found,

outwitted by worm and ant and mosquito,
dawn, dusk, day, night, a dim, edible glow—

Voice Road

I

Voice like the underside of a leaf,
alone, untold . . . and the psychoanalytical
hemlocks darkening this afternoon,
already heartless memory. It takes
a calm to say let happiness
increase me to silence: yet
somewhat past that I speak.

There was an observation
for it, an observation deck.
And boisterous frogs had
melted, when just last spring. . . .
A recollection looks up, the voice
has to put down the voiceless
book it had been forgetfully reading.

2

Night voice like the underside of a bat.

3

Mechanical voice. TWO GALS AND A TRUCK—its crew-cut driver clearing Petersen Park of storm debris, dragging branches by their ends to her pickup while her dog runs, and after the door shuts a voice of steel and gasoline opens.

4

Proper noun voice, illusory diversity, all across Michigan Walt's
Crawlers, here on Kilcherman's Christmas Farm a sign nailed to
a tree: SEE 10,000 POP BOTTLES.

5

Journal voice includes "everything": image, single word, drawings, *pensées,* grocery lists, dates, directions, phone numbers without their names, illegibles, indecipherables. . . .

6

Voices quoted in sequence, that is, randomly, that is, according to the speaker's too-pressed-for-time-to-do-it-any-other-way temperament: "The world is hard on little things," Lillian Gish, *The Night of the Hunter;* "Blessed is the man that walketh not in the counsel of the almighty," Psalms 1:1; "To hate one's native place is more appalling than suicide," James Wright. . . .

7

Sunlight also a voice burning even without its celestial source, draped like a tablecloth on a lakeside picnic table. Planed and bolted in planked parallels. Picnic table steel-chained in case the ghosts return and need a place to anguish. Who almost left all that. Lowercase sunlight on waves alone, voiced continually, voices connected. All those waves ago. How they catch that burning voice and bring it in. How oblong leaves, downed, grounded, station it. Trees bent by wind or disease into question marks that rise out of themselves and answer that voice with crowns of leaves. Glyphs of algae on trunks, a chickadee like a toy ratchet wrench tightening silence somewhere . . . behind . . . the past towards which waves crest . . . it sounds like: one of a million breakable clocks . . . leaves waterwheel from branch to grass in this self-sorry voice . . . without which I walk around the house looking for glasses with a robotic voice gone harmlessly berserk. . . .

8

Yes, one of two gals from TWO GALS AND A TRUCK exactly at her moment of awareness of me, waves ago now, calling her dog back, embarrassed for my being there by her own being or for that matter any being at all.

9

Taking up voice,
   whitecaps beginning out of nowhere . . . memories before you
know it, as ventriloquial,
    as pursued as others,
    you my beloved-you,
    you in a doorway in a St. Kate's T-shirt, whorls over your forehead,
    unfallen Babylon,
    only later to be devastated into the past not by the past but by
the supremely open moment O it needs a little more, a little more,
just to speak.

10

Townes Van Zandt's voice channeling Fred McDowell on a CD, momently past posterity, past death, seriously, scouring out of its ravaged self huge vacancies of space . . . *get ready . . . you gotta move.*

11

Unmoving voice of unmoved picnic tables in sunlight same each in all as picnic tables huddled under a rain shelter, wooden voice chained to the earth, unalarmed as livestock, I'd like to say of the moment, "I'd read a bit, walk about some beach or other," in a voice no less fixed or functional than a table sprayed with leaves . . . I'd like to voice support of their sodden smell, doors of odor to avenues of order, other, mother, father . . . I'd like to speak in a voice set like a table with upturned leaves curled to crone-and-geezer hands of undying memories.

12

Undying voices of formless forms, unorganizable, constitute
the sibyl's waterwork voice, pyrotechnical hydromancy dusky
sunlit waves uncurling *what good are you . . . you are.*

13

One of those days when a vague voice drapes over the lake, eraser of islands and all boundaries between fog and haze, sky and lake, white and gray, gray and blue, wind and waves, suspiration and shudder, inspiration and sigh.

14

at which moment inside the moment did I begin to invite the sense of feeling
accompanied by friends walking along the heartless tide inside the heart of
an emptiness like this on a beach like this where emptiness washes away
ravished by repetitiousness

15

Could it be SPECIFIC, this voice of absence, this *you*? Couldn't I miss *you*?

he said in a failure of feeling.

16

All along the open-ended road inside the moment inside the moment

Open barns open shed doors open apple crates open working farmland field opening inside the opening outside

Down that very road a single voice went so far inside that inside was outside memory

Moronic arrivals brilliant departures average transpersonals

Outside the selfsame lies the selfsame lives still broke forward

A ghost schooner of a moth crawling along night-black window glass soon to be defunct come the autumn blues that changing the heavens change all, stripping trees of their exhibitionist blush then even of their striptease. And when night lifts like the underside of a dead bat curiosity turns over till certain its demise will exert no rabid influence and transform you into a posterity so vampirish it is unlivable simply to contemplate, then it is time to drag one's self up out of sleep, to haunt by being haunted by Voice Road, scenic drive all trees and sunlight-sworded open, road no more steady than this blade of grass the ant travels to the tip of the tip where no tip is and omniscience (nonexistence) beckons, then crawling safely down its sojourn onto a diamonded earth and coterminous along the lifeline of this papery confluence, so many cloudy clouds, so many met and unmet fiends and friends gathered wherever light of day, hearth, or dead-flame lanterns reveal. Today it's a few locals swimming and sunning, two out from shore a bit, looking like a Massacio's Adam and Eve that got out of their shame, yes, still, a bit self-conscious, Banished!, and shorts on him and a suit on her to clothe them for the only way to be in agreement with love is to agree with design. Which is to say another fellow feeling seems out of sorts outside of Empire where Voice Road tracks as far back as ice-scratch, Bar Lake a glacial scion of a far larger glacial body of water, its glacial clouds, glacial trees, two ice-melt lakes, one a sea, one a jewel, two temporary bodies temporarily separated by a gracefully interceding arm of dune, and where it is not bald, wind thrashed grass rooted to such sand-strung influence I would gladly suffer the joy of succumbing to a finalizing influence of elementalism, to such drop-dead continuity, such gorgeously amorphous form, such merciful scattering, settling down, piling, hollowed out at the end of Voice Road, which says we shall be scattered all over creation. Though otherwise it's an ordinary road on which to rejoice crushed gravel, sand, glyphic tire tracks and mud-daubed leaves, impressions from the passage of lovers, friends, tourists, and locals who would be obliged to take any such conjuration of passage as this as lightly as a grain of sand.

Lake Leelanau Goes Still One Day in Fall

The ear wants what it hears to rain in language,
The rain wants images to puddle, flow,
Canoe, thrust paddles through lacustrine looking glass,

Shudder, touched, smoothed beyond sigh
Once flow wins back clarity, that afterlife
That wears its while with absolute unconcern,

Ripples ironed out by transparent cease,
The oldest memoir of language, fluidity
Liquefying sadness, its concentric rings,

The lovely roundness of those spoken vowels,
The vegetal phonemes alive in meadows,
In rooted reveries that obliterate ideals,

Here where fishes fly and clouds congress
With pebble-cobbled bottom worlds
Stocking sky with crappies, trout, and bass,

Undulations leveling to bluest pupil,
Lappings lulled to inaudible lullaby,
Glide of last spring's goslings grown to geese,

Windexed cessation of windrow waves,
Glacial sorrows melted, the bewilderments,
Even the slightest, even the most garrulous

Frog's gargoyle consonants gobbled up,
Gutter-mouthed gutturals, gusts and gales
Gone to glaze, an aimless, amiable gaze,

The furies flatlined to catoptromancy,
Calm and compromise materialized,
Leavetaking leaves loosened from leasehold

Mirrored, and carried by their own reflections.

Under Foot

Casement slant of lake horizon, something's open,
some lit wind getting in to be loved the hell out of,
pushing around everything, it can't get out of the way,
weathered leaves decayed to a venous lace,
unparalyzed first step all of it is walking towards you.
Tin wrappers, rapt, metallic, sun-glint litter.
Cooled hieroglyphics where tires once burned street,
sidewalks sarcoma'd by gum, a goldfinch shadow,
a chance ant, noticeable, discreet, parched for sight.
A foundered upturned fly by an unfurled moth wing
back underfoot for eye to walk on, gull to shit on,
mouth to spit on, light to lean on, eyes to hurt like heaven.
Page of a phone book blown with living names,
Sunday Want Ads, manifestos tersely personal,
bottle caps rusted and tire-flattened to novas,
the child's odd marble cast out like an offending eye,
cigarette filters, cellophane unwrapped, past purpose,
past signification, theory, neglect, past objectification,
past the tragedy that it is a poor thing to have to say so
and that it is a poorer thing not to have to.
Beach pocked and puddles acned by first raindrops,
meadow if you would bloom, marsh if you would sink,
prairie if you would blow away with the sod, embers
if you do not believe in love but only proofs of love,
warm sand if feet are fortunate and bare.
Flat, round, fissured pebbles, their healed shadows,
computer-illiterate grubs and aphids, bee-drilled apples,
ghost apples, revenant bees, invisibles, sublimes,
absences that make the heart beat more erratically
among good eyes, cataracted eyes, closed eyes, open eyes.

All the eyes that ever looked for a place to stand
and stare out of their glare and gaze out of their stare,
water carrying sky all day into the night,
a half-moon's whole light creeping across the lawns.

The Days After the Day of the Dead

A little sunlight every morning now. Gashes of magnesium in graveyard clouds. Breakers blink on and off. Some days have as many as a dozen twilights and that many dawns and that many midnights and that many noons. Other days shake off sunlight in cascades until they are free of the burden of eyesight. And there are days of wind that are like years, and there are days that are like grass bleached to an almost dead language all at once stilled so that only the light can be said to move, and just barely. There are shorter days that are cinders, and even shorter days when the only colors are blue, green, gray, chalk, sediment, and chromium, as if the rest of the rainbow had been emptied into the kitchen sink. I have had days stare back at me as if to say, let's see who will darken first. For the strangest days of all are hemlocks in the midst of yellow beech. Their darkness is so alive that any light at all seems an insupportable belief, all so the blackest winter nights can have a place year-round. These days are not only inevitable but possible, as old and fatal as childhood.

Sand Theory

Sieving through all and any manner of grasping it
no matter how tightly cupped the hands and fingers,
it comes down to no more lies, only precious goodbyes,

only the time to say what the future can pray
while waves like dunes themselves flatline to transparence,
and grass blades stream then rest in light, October blond,

comprising the look of what this sand would do
if it could escape itself and shine in wind
and uptick a little above earth while the days shuffle.

It is shifty, untrustworthy, almost no world
beneath the feet themselves almost not feet,
it gets into the car and it is driven away

but it doesn't vanish, not now, not by a long shot.
Two three-feet salmon are heaving mildly by the grass.
The father smokes and casts another line,

his child mats their tails with rot-spotted maple leaves
as if to prepare them for the rest of their journey.
Our destinations the ones we understand the least,

another fall day, another, along the Traverse, now
under the overpass where cars like censors spread
a heavenly toxicity and while I'm walking into all my dusks

maybe the patterning of days like sand creates
the promise of an elsewhere, luminous night
beyond real so we don't have to bother to look back—

gulls on seasick lake swell like studious burls,
judicial on the canine stumps of a ghost weir—
maybe all sightings catch and brain the life out of the instant.

And if I could shuffle all days into one divine day
the sand might settle to the same distinctions,
vacant horizons, sometimes the inchworm tanker

at which I choose to wave, though to its ship hands
I am a part of everything invisible.
And then the tanker isn't there just one hour later,

and then night clouds piling up behind North Manitou,
varicose with lightning, and whatever ghosts
gather behind my eyes to gaze out my stares

include both dead and living, and yet I mostly miss myself,
I turn myself away each night and day
while combers unroll scrolls that break all ties.

Place is on the move, grain by grain, no chaff,
grit in the teeth, no wings, no golden modesty,
no mysterious lives, no unnamed poor.

It hardly matters which day wind picks it up.
It gets into the ears, it abrades the retina,
it gets into pockets and shoes and underwear,

it has no face and it has no idea it has no face,
it has no eyes to see it has no eyes,
it has no ears to be told it has no ears.

It is neither memory nor clairvoyance.
I do not think it any different than midnight sky,
black sediment of night pitted with stars

shining so inaudibly that we think all light
is voiceless, until a new day dawns with bluffs
we might call headlands if these balding heads

weren't swimming with such wind-duned mindlessness,
dandered in leaf fall blown beyond beyond,
leaves themselves degenerate with macula—

like failing eyes in some ophthalmologist's office
of absolute information that passes for vision.
Nancy's been here a week, then she leaves again.

And then the almost ceremonial sobbing—
we might both be sobbing piles of sand
and why not, after all it has been everything,

it was a rope in Herbert's hand, it was pyramids,
it was a sphinx, it was a house, a church,
a bank, a stadium, a city, dead streets, sand kids crying sand.

It gathers but at such moments is all departure.
And even so it's still far more actual
than "teardown" McMansions hung with curtain-free windows.

No one can afford to live in some of them any longer,
their living rooms you can see right through, to lake,
not even ghosts show up at their windows, only sand.

For it is to be walked upon and lain upon
and it is also to be buggied and bulldozed.
Sometimes it is in the lake, sometimes it is below the lake,

sometimes above the lake and in the wind and at the face—
a creepy integrity, it is totality
when you are in it, surrounded by it, when

its dunes block any view of the life that defies it,
even though it gathers as if it were also living.
I wish it were, I'd have myself a world in it.

Instead I see the whole wide universe
not in a grain of sand but as a grain of sand.
I see myself disturb it with every step.

For it flees the earthly places of greatest disruption.
And then it reaccumulates and buries
entire villages and farms and orchards and families.

And yet always it leads to day, and green on lake
this late chill fall day manifests some warmth,
sky so deep blue the blues blue beyond sorrow,

cedars so shadowy blackness looks alive and well.
No doubt it has no will but it can be suffocating
because it has no real choice, whereas . . .

it is, if nothing else, grammatical, the most
disparate ellipsis in the history of language,
the inundating lake off Sleeping Bear

its absence, its absence a presence it bears on its back—
accumulation of a bewildering wilderness,
light so filtered through clouds, so refracted,

so shadowed by cloud and so reflective of cloud
that all there is to see is impossible
to source except to say that the darker patches

on lake may be reflections of darker clouds—
unless these very reflections are the very shadows of
these darker clouds . . . shadow and reflection

merge to such brilliance as blows away contemplation.
Of the two skies: one to fall in, one to fly in. . . .
Above, below, dune grass now blond-brown-

sandpainted, an image of the sand it holds to.
And what it holds to, holds it fast and together,
as the lake that seems to hover above the earth

collects and deepens without loves or loss.
The dunes mime some justice of waving waves goodbye,
the lake is the ghost of a glacier, the clouds

are the ghosts of lakes, their rains the ghosts of clouds.
Sand posits its pronouns if only to farewells,
days and days know not whereof sand speaks,

phrase after worldly phrase ghosting the world,
salutations and growing distances.
Each dune, real, preexisting justice,

its own profile, profuse, diffuse, scatters
and blows away only because it gathers.
Dusk, now, tiniest corrugations on lake,

pebbles showing from under, in cloudlight, to cloudlight,
in clarity, with clarity, as these clouds
gather the light of all the sunny days.

Pebbles, and shells, and sand, a grave bottom
stays under this clear water too icy to touch.
Yet even a ghost would wish for all of this,

pay homage not just to human consciousness,
and not to his god or his nature or to his poetry,
but to this wholly-out-in-the-openness,

grass smoothed low by wind, wind combed by grass,
fire soothing water, rain pitting beach,
sand humanized by footprints broken and deserted

till nearly formless. Then sand fills in the forms.
Night, now, navigable quintessentia of the stars,
impossible to separate the dead from the living,

up there if not down here, the absences,
the presences that sooner than later will be absences—
the homeless homes will be haunted by it,

the insoluble where, its irresolvable voices.

Leaf Watching, for Landor

Milkweed tickling nose and ears,
this is November
a day or two after

the day of the dead.
Orange cap on head
so small-gamers

won't take me for prey,
more and more I give to joy,
my yearly narrowing,

ghosts around the fire,
fewer and fewer tourist cars,
birds seen and unseen,

shambles of crimson.
The leaves are falling,
torrid ghost money,

currency all wind,
or hanging, crepitating,
a loose change

as beautiful to lose
as ever it is to win,
blown away again, again.

Essay on Craft

1

Creation requires some sense of the casual because no one wakes
formally.

2

The land always dawns on itself, but we never wake to ourselves.

3

Acorns drop like thrown dice to the deck, then scutter a brief while, like
failed tops, then nothing falling down there, then, as always, a few more.

4

Minor grievances are doubly unnerving because they seem to signify that
our suffering is just as minor.

5

Hope, in any case, seems firmly isolated from its staggering circumstances.

6

The rich, verdant pageantry of the senses only renders the words that much more arid and blank and severe.

7

Mother-loss and father-loss turn out to be actually two of the more cozy corners in a filthy raucous jailhouse of all loss.

8

As for comic omissions, who cares what the names were and whose faces glowed like moons at curtain call but the people out there,

9

who only had a handful of decades to step inside?

10

Desire, appeal, friendship, safety in numbers.

11

But there's fear here and there the world around, and some challenge far greater than those posed by either popularity or loneliness or infotainment.

12

I try to summon it all the time in a way that doesn't serve mean purposes.

13

That is, I try to tell it what to do.

14

It is not always a kind relationship. There are moments when kindness is not called for, and the truth that this is so makes kindness itself seem spectral and purposeless and out of sorts.

15

I tell you that I don't always feel an express purpose, sometimes there is nothing before me.

16

What does it mean that words can be lined up to best the best and leave the illiterate to die?

17

What does it mean that you have to slow down to get anywhere? What if you stopped moving altogether?

18

Then this: this: we must place it here even if we are blind to the outcome, even if we never know the person who might have been seeking the same space in time, even if we never meet.

First Bible

A beat-up King James split into sheaves themselves
Tattered, paper so old it crisps. To you I did this. . . .

Binding broken, this keepsake in among typing paper,
Books shuffled, Genesis on bottom, New Testament

Between Kings and Lamentations, studied to its ruin,
Dog-eared Babylon, scattered ancestors, their terrors,

The dust they kissed and cursed, prayers they fumbled,
Passing tribes and marriages and deliquescing glories

Fouled up, mishandled, soiled to this yellowing end.
Creation, revelation, kingdom I thumbed through so,

Shattered, fallen apart, gardens and deserts and cities,
Why more of this? Did we multiply to compassion?

What on earth is such abundance, mutilated friend?
Miracle, language, did I love what I love to this mess?

Pestilence, drought, disease, yes, I shall dearly miss
You, a black keepsake that says night shall be light,

You psalms, prophesies, bread broken, bodies, nations,
Crumbs of crumbs so crushed it leaves me breathless.

Those Yachts

Those yachts like lit-up slices of wedding cake—
the further light departs from dark the more decadent it gets.
    They wait for night to shed the dunes and waters
altogether,
        they make the stars seem almost to shy away,
        they prey on the last of the failing eyesight of every man,
animal, and shade,
        they smoke their pipes and tap them empty
        into the lake that bears them on its back.

—

    They stay too long in my field of vision, which is a lake,
they welcome the impending dark,
        they sweetly believe in a malicious universe,
        they cling to an evil father-belief,
        they wait for some retributive totality
        to erase the doves and the woodpeckers and the cardinals
and branches that in a breeze have that wooden give as if
        every moment of their existence
        some alit bird had from its grasp
        just released that branch and taken wing.

—

    Yet they fail to crush the spirit or the fact
    because in their buoyant leadenness

they fail miserably to appreciate
that every blade of grass presses upon the firmament,
    that eternity is the mother of clichés,
    that grief is good and pronounced incompletion,
    that night will put each star dead or alive
before us and above us without daring to snuff a single one.

—

Eyes snail across such spans as these, and perhaps
saying so casts the shadow of heaven
    like punishment across those yachts.
    And sends them into oblivion.
    But then this dream of justice subsides,
    and their glamorous lights appear again.
    It is twilight and soon not even mirrors will give
sunlight back,
    not even their cousins the lakes and rivers
will scramble it,
    not even books will talk it back to life.

—

And all those yachts can do is flourish idly,
    and for all the money in the world they cannot see the light,
    or a lake that turns the last of it away by reflecting it thinly
and with as much thrift as possible,
    or the stars that refuse to keep it,
    or the moon that borrows it,
    or the dim sand that holds its living heat.

The Last White-Throated Sparrow of May

Such depths as can be sounded only at heights. It goes like this and this and this voice of a straw all the while the profiles of the dunes scatter. These profiles may be signatures, lineaments, ancestral and monumental, but they all scatter. Meanwhile, like every bird on earth this last straggler, most of the time, remains quiet. But when it breaks the silence it makes one and one and one and one, etc., glad and sorry that all of this must be given thanks, must be written just so. O, we will find fault with paradise. It rebukes us. Its aspen speak without having to stop in the distance to hear themselves back there, like a stand of Eurydices. Being here a little while would seem to be a matter of staying still and being in motion or staying still and watching, or vocalizing earth from the highest reaches of a dead cedar all the way across a shore and over a lake where no tree roots, no nests hold. This is the sound of the last white throat of the woods and this is going to stop far short of any return to its origin, far short of any original farewell. This is ever beyond saying so, beyond song.

Waking Slow

You don't know if dawns are the only afterlives,
the whole thing still a little fuzzy but already
the trees sharpening, windows gleaming messages,
leaves that reach out cleaving to a green disregard,
far-off wars imagination cannot even fathom
real again and our newspapers unfolding
with such rapidity their casualties and distractions
when you sigh you hear someone other than you,
you stand alongside your choices in your nice house
and it is as if the entire universe were sighing
like grief had something to do with everything,
even you, who helped make all this up just this way
you think you find all things to be that can't change,
summoned at last into paralysis steadfast and clear.
And yet even if it is affliction to think you can
and must love all of the most despicable of it,
here you are at the beginning of another morning
thrown together inside so many spiralings,
so many soaring worries that you can't help but feel
that the angels never even needed their wings,
that specifically the two who brought you here
are raising their arms to you and taking you
inside a circle once everything is, yet again, too late,
both being here and one of them see-through,
though they are also not here for you at all,
you a hereafter of many having loved each other
and their faith in time, which forgave everything.